Gods

Zeus – *king of the gods*

Hera – *his wife*

Athena – *goddess of wisdom and warfare*

Aphrodite – *goddess of love*

Apollo – *god of poetry and music*

Ate – *blindness-inducing daughter of Zeus*

Hephaestus – *craftsman god*

Hermes – *messenger god*

Poseidon – *god of the sea, father of the Cyclops Polyphemus*

Series 117

This is a Ladybird Expert book, one of a series of titles for an adult readership. Written by some of the leading lights and outstanding communicators in their fields and published by one of the most trusted and well-loved names in books, the Ladybird Expert series provides clear, accessible and authoritative introductions, informed by expert opinion, to key subjects drawn from science, history and culture.

Every effort has been made to ensure images are correctly attributed, however if any omission or error has been made please notify the Publisher for correction in future editions.

MICHAEL JOSEPH

UK | USA | Canada | Ireland | Australia
India | New Zealand | South Africa

Michael Joseph is part of the Penguin Random House group of companies whose addresses can be found at global.penguinrandomhouse.com

First published 2019

001

Text copyright © Daisy Dunn, 2019
All images copyright © Ladybird Books Ltd, 2019
The moral right of the author has been asserted

Printed in Italy by L.E.G.O. S.p.A.

A CIP catalogue record for this book is available from the British Library

ISBN: 978–0–718–18828–3

www.greenpenguin.co.uk

Penguin Random House is committed to a sustainable future for our business, our readers and our planet. This book is made from Forest Stewardship Council® certified paper.

Homer

Daisy Dunn

with illustrations by
Angelo Rinaldi

Ladybird Books Ltd, London

The epic poems

Homer's epics, the *Iliad* and the *Odyssey*, are two of the most influential works of literature in the world. Completed in Greek in the eighth or early seventh century BCE, they represent a milestone in the history of civilization but are above all exquisite stories, which can tell us as much about who we are and might become as about who we were.

The eighth century BCE was a time of great change in the Greek world. It saw the birth of the Olympic Games, the construction of the first temples to the gods, and the rediscovery of the art of writing with the invention of a new alphabet. The Greeks were beginning to travel widely overseas and establish settlements in places such as Sicily.

Homer's epics reflect these new developments, despite being set some 400 years earlier, in the Late Bronze Age. But they also feel very ancient, because they contain traces of language and myths which predate them by generations. Homer's first audiences would already have been familiar with a myth in which Paris, prince of Troy, judged Aphrodite, goddess of love, to be the most beautiful deity. As his reward, Paris ran away with Helen of Sparta. Her husband, Menelaus, and brother-in-law, Agamemnon, responded by leading a mighty Greek army against Troy (also known as 'Ilios' or 'Ilion').

The Trojan War is Homer's theme. The *Iliad*, the older of the two poems by perhaps forty years, describes over a month in the tenth and final year of the conflict. Its sequel, the *Odyssey*, follows the journey of Odysseus, the last man to return home. Together, the epics have reverberated down the centuries as tantalizing relics of a world half real, half imagined.

Who was Homer?

Homer's identity is a mystery. Most people in antiquity believed that he was the author of both epics, but they had only theories about what he might have been like. The word '*homeros*' meant 'hostage' in Greek, so some pictured Homer as a captive, but it could also mean 'blind'. The idea of a blind bard was particularly attractive because the *Odyssey* features a blind poet named Demodocus.

Seven ancient cities claimed Homer for their own. Was he a man of Smyrna (Izmir in Turkey)? Did he come from Ios in the Cyclades, where he is said to be buried? Did he live on the rocky Aegean island of Chios? The Chian connection is perhaps the strongest. The location of Chios is described with great accuracy in the *Odyssey*, and rhapsodes calling themselves 'Homeridae' ('children of Homer') performed the poems on the island from as early as the sixth century BCE.

It is now considered highly likely that the poems originated on the west coast of Turkey or in the eastern Aegean. This region, known as Ionia, incorporated Chios and Smyrna. The language of Homer's poems is broadly Ionic, but layered with archaisms and traces of dialects from other parts of the Greek world as well.

In 1897, the writer Samuel Butler argued that the *Odyssey* was authored by a woman. Scholars had long been debating whether a real Homer had even existed. While some did believe that each poem could only have been the product of a single mind, others suspected that the works took shape over time in the minds of several poets, or represented amalgamations of many earlier versions.

The oral tradition

A breakthrough came in the twentieth century, when American scholar Milman Parry showed that there lay behind Homer an 'oral tradition'. This meant that it was possible for the poetry, composed without writing, to be preserved by being memorized and recited, passed down from bard to bard.

Parry found evidence for this in the poems' structure and song-like rhythm. Each line is a 'hexameter', formed of six sections, like the bars of a music score. Some bars contain a long sound followed by two short ones: 'dum di di'. Others – and almost always the last bar in each line – consist of two long sounds: 'dum dum'. The poet also repeats passages, as a singer would a chorus, and certain phrases, such as 'rose-fingered Dawn', 'unharvested sea' and 'godlike Odysseus'. As a bard performed the stories, he could hone them, incorporating stock phrases like these wherever he needed to fill a bar, adding new words while maintaining very old ones. Homer's is consequently a Greek that no one ever spoke. Through both accident and design, it sounds older than it is, which is why deciphering its origins is so difficult.

There may still have been a 'Homer', a mastermind who shaped the inherited material into the complete *Iliad*, and perhaps a second 'Homer' who did the same for the *Odyssey*. Both are coherent works of literature and must have been perfected when written down in the eighth or early seventh century BCE. Whether we prefer to think of 'Homer' as a master editor or as a blind bard who first came up with the stories generations earlier, or as simply a label for the *Iliad* and *Odyssey*, song remains central to the epics. Even the fearsome Greek warrior Achilles sings of men's glorious deeds to the accompaniment of a lyre.

The evidence for a Trojan War

The ancients mostly believed that there really was a war at Troy and archaeologists have long been searching for the evidence. In the 1870s, a wealthy Prussian businessman named Heinrich Schliemann was told of an ancient site on the west coast of modern Turkey. Although he had no archaeological training, Schliemann had always dreamed of finding Troy, so he travelled to the site at Hissarlik and began to dig. He found some jewellery and other treasures, which turned out to be around a thousand years too old to have come from Homer's Troy. Schliemann had dug too deep.

He had, however, excavated the right location. Most archaeologists now agree that Hissarlik is indeed former Troy. Its geographical position between Greece and the Black Sea would have made it a desirable place to sack. The Hittites, an ancient people centred at Hattusas (Bogazkale, central Turkey), have even left behind inscriptions which hint at historic conflicts over Bronze Age Troy. Homer's epics may well have been coloured by stories which evolved from many wars. And while no firm evidence of the war Homer described has yet emerged, Hissarlik, with its citadel and plain, bears some resemblance to the Troy of the poems.

Archaeologists have identified nine main historical settlements in its layers, of which the most developed were the sixth and seventh. 'Troy VI', which existed between 1750 and 1300 BCE, the period before Homer's Trojan War, had enormous limestone fortification walls and towers. In the *Iliad*, too, a 'wide and very beautiful wall' surrounds Troy, built, according to the sea god Poseidon, 'so that their city might be indestructible'. The name Hissarlik means 'Place of Fortresses' in Turkish.

The Mycenaeans

Some of Homer's descriptions of Troy also call to mind
a real civilization known as the Mycenaean. Famous as
inventors of an early form of writing known as Linear B,
the Mycenaeans built luxurious palaces in the Peloponnese
at places such as Tiryns, Pylos and Mycenae, from which
they took their name. Although the Mycenaeans flourished
before Homer's time, in 1600–1200 BCE, we may see the
influence of their palace culture on his descriptions in the
Iliad. The palace of the Trojan King Priam, for example, is
'surpassingly beautiful, furnished with polished porticoes'
and 'fifty rooms of polished stone'.

Mycenae is mentioned in the *Iliad* as the kingdom of
the leader of the Greek army, Agamemnon. It is, says
Homer, 'abundant in gold'. So the amateur archaeologist
Heinrich Schliemann found when he excavated some of
the graves there in the nineteenth century. Among his
finds was a splendid gold mask belonging to a man with a
wide face, large beard and long nose. The so-called 'Mask
of Agamemnon' is in fact around 400 years older than
the Agamemnon of Homer's poems but well evokes the
splendour of his kingdom.

The world Homer presented in his epics, with its palaces and
'well-laid streets', its bronze and gold, was partly inspired by
his vision of what Mycenaean life was like. While he used
artistic licence to create his portrait of Troy, his epics contain
distant memories of Mycenaean culture and descriptions
informed by the splendid monuments it left behind, some of
which – intricate round tombs, impressively high walls and
an iconic Lion Gate – can still be seen at Mycenae today.

The 'Dark Age'

The Mycenaeans were long gone by the time Homer was composing his epics. Their civilization collapsed in the twelfth century BCE. The mysterious demise of the Mycenaeans is sometimes attributed to famine or an invasion of Greek-speaking peoples from the north, the Dorians. There followed what is often called a Greek Dark Age, in which the population dwindled and skills such as writing, which the Mycenaeans had cultivated, were forgotten.

The collapse of the Mycenaean civilization occurred at around the same time as a fire broke out at the site of ancient Troy. Archaeologists believe that Hissarlik burned in roughly 1180 BCE. According to the calculations of an ancient mathematician named Eratosthenes, the Trojan War took place in 1184/3 BCE. In the *Iliad* the day is envisaged when the Greeks will set Troy ablaze. The discovery of arrowheads at the site supports the theory of a conflict. It is possible that the fire at Hissarlik was the result of warfare, and that the destruction of the citadel, whether by war or natural disaster, inspired Homer's story of the Trojan War.

We may never know the truth, but the *Iliad* might even have been composed as an explanation for the period of decline that ensued from around 1150 BCE. Homer's epics mark the end of this so-called Dark Age. By the eighth century BCE many Greeks had migrated to Ionia, the probable birthplace of Homer's epics. It was soon after they developed the Greek alphabet and art of writing that they first wrote the poems down.

Golden Age thinking

Homer portrayed the men of his epics as mightier than those of his own time. His poems are populated by sons of gods and mortals who heave enormous boulders on to their shoulders, shoot arrows with unerring precision and feast on hearty portions of mutton, pork and goat roasted on spits, even in wartime.

But just as Homer imagined the warriors of the Late Bronze Age to be superior to the men who came after them, so the warriors in the poems tend to imagine that their ancestors were superior to themselves. One of the old men fighting for the Greeks, Nestor, has lived through three generations. He tells his allies that none of them could conquer the great men he once knew. Agamemnon, the Greek leader, takes great pleasure in telling his junior Diomedes that he is inferior to his father, who fought at Thebes. (This earlier conflict was the subject of an epic poem that some ancient authors attributed to Homer.) Even so, Diomedes can lift a stone so heavy that not even two men in Homer's time could carry it. And, astonishingly, he wounds the goddess Aphrodite with his spear.

Homer's genius is to show us that, no matter how good the times we live in, we shall always view the past as a relative golden age. It is telling that even Alexander the Great kept a copy of the *Iliad* under his pillow and read it while on campaign.

The *Iliad* – the feud

Part of what makes the *Iliad* so timeless is the simplicity of
its plot, which develops out of a feud between two people.
Agamemnon has taken a concubine, and when he refuses to
give her up in return for a ransom from her father, a priest
of Apollo, the god sends a plague of arrows upon the Greek
army. A prophet tells Agamemnon that they will continue to
suffer until he relinquishes the girl. Reluctantly, Agamemnon
agrees to do so, but demands another gift in recompense.
One of his most capable soldiers, fair-haired Achilles,
suggests he wait until they sack Troy to select a new war
prize. The dispute quickly escalates and Agamemnon seizes
Achilles' own captive woman, Briseis.

The *Iliad* begins with the words: 'Sing, Muse, of the
destructive wrath of Peleus' son Achilles'. Homer's is a
world in which possessions matter, and not simply for their
material worth. When Agamemnon takes away Achilles'
woman, he tramples on his honour, and this sets the tone
for the rest of the poem. Achilles feels the slight all the
more sorely because he knows that he is destined to die
young. His father, Peleus, is mortal but his mother, Thetis,
is a goddess of the sea. In his sorrow Achilles asks her
to persuade Zeus, king of the gods, to help the opposing
Trojans succeed in the war until Agamemnon realizes the
mistake he has made.

The gods and fate

Homer's gods are forever meddling in human affairs. They take sides on the battlefield, knock spears out of men's hands, destroy their fortifications. Apollo batters the Greeks' wall 'with great ease, as a boy does a sandcastle by the shore'. An ancient critic said that Homer made his men gods and his gods men. The divinities bicker over the direction of the war, then simply return to feasting on the heights of Mount Olympus.

In the first of the twenty-four books of the *Iliad*, it is revealed that it was Zeus' will that Achilles' wrath should cause the deaths of many of his comrades. Homer was probably familiar with an ancient story that Zeus caused the Trojan War in order to solve the problem of overpopulation. Homer nonetheless preferred to place the blame for the war on the mortals and the gods, whom the mortals in turn blame for their own mistakes. Later in the *Iliad*, for example, Agamemnon claims that his quarrel with Achilles and the carnage it caused were not his fault. Zeus, Fate and the vengeful goddesses cast '*ate*' or 'blindness' upon him, he says, when he took away Achilles' woman.

Ate, daughter of Zeus, is said to wander above men's heads, filling them with delusion. Zeus is the author of men's fates but is himself beholden to an overarching fate. He has a responsibility to maintain order on Olympus. This means that, though he is king of the gods, he cannot always have his way. To his deepest sorrow he must accept what is fated and let his mortal son Sarpedon die in the war.

Death

Much of the drama of Homer derives from the fact that very few characters can anticipate a pleasant afterlife. In the *Odyssey*, Menelaus is told he will go to the idyllic 'Elysian Field' when he dies, but most men fight to the death only to wander the underworld of Hades as senseless 'phantoms of the mortal dead'.

Death itself is cruel and unpitying in the epics. It pushes mighty warriors to the ground until they are clutching at the dust. A spear goes through a soldier's groin and he bellows like an animal. The landscape of Troy intrudes upon his corpse, waves lapping it until 'both eels and fish make busy around him, feeding upon and devouring the fat around his kidneys'.

Death is no gentler on men fathered by gods. Zeus' son Sarpedon succumbs to the force of Achilles' closest friend, Patroclus, whose spear strikes him 'where the diaphragm is close by the pounding heart'. As Sarpedon falls, he is likened to an oak tree, white poplar or tall pine, felled by men for ship timber.

Homeric epic is rich in extended similes which make even the most sorrowful events sound beautiful. When one of the Trojan King Priam's sons dies, it is said he 'dropped his head to one side like the stalk of a poppy in the garden, weighed down by its seeds and spring showers: so his head nodded to one side beneath the weight of his helmet'.

Greeks vs Trojans

Homer often drew comparisons with the natural world, as if to make what was strange and unintelligible more familiar and relatable. Similes inspired by nature also enabled him to draw a subtle yet powerful distinction between the Greeks and the Trojans. In the *Iliad*, for example, the Trojans enter battle 'like sheep which stand in the stables of a very rich man, countless, producing white milk, bleating unceasingly as they listen to the voices of their lambs'. They speak many different languages because they 'were called from many different lands'. The Greeks, by contrast, who historically called themselves 'Hellenes' but are variously referred to as 'Argives', 'Achaeans' and 'Danaans' in the poems, proceed in silence. They tend to be characterized as more stately than the Trojans.

Comparisons such as these are important because they give an impression of how the war has developed since Paris ran off with Helen almost a decade earlier. The Greeks are focused and resolute because they are no longer fighting over her alone. The war has escalated and their hearts are now set on absolute victory. So Agamemnon declares that not one of the Trojans must escape destruction, 'not even a boy a mother carries in her womb'. The Trojans have been on the defensive from the start. Even when Zeus is assisting them, they often seem less stalwart than the Greeks. Through his descriptions, Homer cleverly foreshadows the fate that awaits them.

The hero's renown

The Homeric hero displays a particular set of character traits. He is not only courageous and strong but motivated by a desire for '*kleos*' – a glorious and immortal reputation. While he is mindful of how he is perceived in his own time, it is the possibility of being remembered for generations after his death that drives him. The immortality of Homer's poems only perpetuates their message that though man is ephemeral, his name and deeds need not be.

If Paris falls short of the heroic ideal, then his brother Hector represents almost everything a hero should be. In one scene he berates Paris for his folly and lust while the other Trojans are fighting for his sake. When leopard-skin-clad Paris does succeed in striking a Greek with an arrow, the blow is likened to that inflicted by a woman or a child. By now Helen can hardly stand him – or herself. Wishing she were with a better man, she calls herself 'a horrid, evil-scheming bitch'. She knows that she and the 'blindness' of Paris are to blame for the war. It is their folly, not their renown, that will be sung about for years to come.

Unlike Paris, Hector is driven by '*thumos*', a passionate fighting spirit, as well as the desire for '*kleos*'. He thinks of his honour but also of his family. In one tender scene he visits his wife, Andromache, and their baby son, Astyanax. As the infant recoils at the sight of his bronze, horse-hair plumed helmet, Hector and Andromache laugh. It is a rare moment of comedy. Enslavement awaits them should the Greeks triumph. Achilles has already killed Andromache's father and seven brothers and sacked her homeland.

Persuading Achilles

The turning point in the poem comes when, with Apollo's help, Hector kills the soldier Patroclus, who was dressed in the armour of his closest companion, Achilles. Until then, Achilles has hung back from the fighting, smarting at his maltreatment by Agamemnon. Three of his most persuasive allies, Odysseus, Ajax and Phoenix, have tried to induce him to fight, offering him Agamemnon's choice of gifts: tripods, gold, horses, women (including Briseis), and the opportunity to be his son-in-law. But Achilles has rejected them all as unworthy of him.

Only the desire to avenge the death of Patroclus can persuade him to join battle. Overcome by grief and anger, Achilles decides to fight, and in doing so demonstrates what it means to make the ultimate choice. The tension in this moment contributes to the power of Homer's *Iliad*. Achilles must fight Hector face-to-face and defeat him. But as Achilles' mother has warned him, he will die soon after Hector. Achilles goes ahead even though he knows it means his own death. He chooses a short but distinguished life over a long and unremarkable one.

But what of Hector? His father warns him that he will die if he fights Achilles. But Hector feels an intense form of shame before the Trojans because he believes he ought to have led them back into the city sooner to save them. If Achilles' decision is difficult, then so is Hector's. Homer presents them as dramatic counterparts, different but united by the difficulty of their choices.

The battle

While describing only a short period in the Trojan War,
Homer provides an impression of the wider conflict
culminating in the mighty battle between Hector, the
greatest hero among the Trojans, and Achilles, the greatest
hero among the Greeks. Their duel is the signal event of the
Iliad and presages the end of the war itself.

Homer paints a magnificently vivid picture of each stage in
the battle. Achilles appears in armour made by the craftsman
god Hephaestus. Hector trembles and runs. Achilles chases.
Zeus looks on and half-heartedly wonders whether the
gods might save Hector. Athena darts down from Olympus
to assist Achilles. Apollo protects Hector. But then Zeus
balances the fates of the soldiers in his scales; Hector's
sinks. He must die. Apollo leaves. Athena stays.

Hector reaches for his sword but Achilles charges and
drives his spear into his neck. Hector begs Achilles to return
his body to the Trojans so that it is not eaten by the dogs.
Achilles will not. He calls Hector a dog and wishes he could
eat him himself. The image of dogs pervades the *Iliad*,
evoking the terrible fate that awaits a man whose corpse
remains exposed. Earlier in the poem, Hector in the heat of
battle was even described as rabid.

With his dying breath, Hector accurately predicts Achilles'
coming death, which will occur when Apollo guides Paris'
arrow into his heel. Untroubled, Achilles strips Hector of
his armour. The Greeks gather to stab his corpse. Achilles
bores through Hector's feet to tie him to his chariot and drag
him through the dust. Homer spares no details of the abuse.
He isolates Achilles from us as well as from his compatriots
while illustrating his strength.

The Trojan horse

Homer in fact strikes a careful balance between admiring the heroism of his warriors and portraying the agony of the conflict. No glorifier of war, he provides in the closing books of the *Iliad* the most harrowing portrait of the devastation endured on both sides. While Hector's wife faints, his father, Priam, rolls in dung and his mother, Hecuba, weeps, Zeus issues a message. Achilles is to give up Hector's corpse to Priam in exchange for gifts. In a moving scene, Priam takes Achilles by the knees and kisses his hands – the hands which have killed so many of his sons – and asks for his pity. The men are united in remembrance for their losses.

The *Iliad* closes with Hector's funeral. It is only in the *Odyssey* that we learn how the Greeks finally prevailed over the Trojans. Concealed within an enormous wooden horse, devised by Odysseus, the Greeks entered the citadel by stealth to unleash their devastation and bring the Trojans to surrender. Odysseus kept his comrades silent inside his clever contraption when they were eager to call out.

Menelaus, the cuckolded husband of Helen, tells of Odysseus' endurance. In the *Odyssey*, he is back in Sparta with Helen by his side. His brother Agamemnon, meanwhile, survived the war only to be murdered on his return to Mycenae by the lover his wife had taken in his absence. Agamemnon's son, Orestes, then killed his father's murderer in revenge. This story, told only briefly in Homer, inspired some of the greatest plays of the fifth century BCE.

Odysseus of Ithaca

The *Odyssey* recounts the adventures of Odysseus during his lengthy journey home after the end of the war. At 12,110 lines, the poem is slightly shorter than the *Iliad* (15,693 lines). It is also the younger of the two epics and in some ways the more ornate. It serves as a lively sequel to the story of the Trojan War.

From Troy, Odysseus must strive to reach Ithaca. This 'far-seen' island has never convincingly been identified, but is said in the poem to lie near Zakynthos, Same and Doulichion, which are islands in the Ionian Sea. Odysseus reveals that Ithaca is 'rugged, but a kind nurse to men' and has a mountain that 'quivers with foliage'. It may not have been the prettiest place but Odysseus could 'recognize no other land sweeter'. It was home.

While Odysseus has been away, his faithful wife, Penelope, has been resisting the advances of 108 suitors, who sit around playing draughts, feasting on the livestock and plotting to kill the prince, Telemachus. Penelope has said that she will remarry only when she has finished weaving a funeral shroud for Laertes, Odysseus' father, for when he dies. Cunningly unpicking her threads at night, she has put off a wedding for over three years when one of her serving women reveals her secret to the callous suitors. Penelope will have to marry one of them soon.

An island nymph

Little do they know in Ithaca that Odysseus is still alive.
He has spent the last seven years on the island of Ogygia
(probably Gozo, just off Malta) with a beautiful nymph
called Calypso. Names are often significant in Homer's
poems. 'Calypso' comes from the Greek for 'to conceal', the
implication being that she is closeting Odysseus from his
homecoming while he is unaware of her enchantment. He is
explicitly said to sleep with her 'by necessity' and 'against
his will' in caves surrounded by cypress trees, fountains and
trailing grape vines.

His predicament may not sound particularly terrible but
Odysseus is miserable when we first meet him. He has
navigated a dangerous passage between a six-headed
monster named Scylla and a whirlpool called Charybdis
before arriving on this beautiful island. And yet, living up to
his name, which is linked to the Greek for 'pain' and 'hate',
he spends his days sitting on the beach, looking out to sea
and weeping for home.

In the first book of the *Odyssey*, Zeus complains that men
are always blaming the gods for their troubles when in fact
their worries stem from their own indiscretions. His words
here ring true, for we learn that Odysseus came to Calypso's
island alone after the last of his men perished. He has lost
many men over the course of his homecoming, but these
particular allies died as a result of eating the cattle of the
sun god, which they had been forbidden to touch. Isolated
by his virtue and rare piety towards the gods, Odysseus cuts
a pitiable figure. It is in recognition of these attributes that
Zeus and his daughter Athena agree Odysseus should reach
his home.

The Telemachy

There's another reason why Odysseus should return to Ithaca. His son, Telemachus, has not seen his father for so long that he has begun to doubt his own paternity. Unable to fend off his mother's suitors by himself, Telemachus is in dire need of Odysseus. The first four books of the *Odyssey* are known as the 'Telemachy' because they describe Telemachus embarking on a journey of his own. His quest is prompted by the goddess Athena, who arrives in the disguise of a mortal man and bids him to confront the suitors and travel to Pylos and Sparta in search of news of his father. The journey will give him confidence and purpose. She tells him that she believes Odysseus will be home soon.

The Telemachy also enables Homer to reveal the legacy and aftermath of the Trojan War through the eyes of the survivors. At Sparta, for example, Telemachus finds Menelaus hosting a wedding feast for his children. His daughter is betrothed to a son of Achilles. His son by a slave woman is to marry a Spartan girl. This joyous scene, in which neighbours dine, a lyrist plays and a pair of acrobats leads the dancing, segues to sorrow as the conversation turns to the war. Menelaus and Telemachus become so tearful that Helen feels compelled to spike their wine with an Egyptian potion to make them forget their woes. But the meeting also provides hope, for Menelaus tells Telemachus that he has heard from a truthful old deity of the sea that Odysseus is alive and being detained on an island by Calypso.

Navigating the sea

The gods play as important a role in the *Odyssey* as they do in the *Iliad*. They both assist and hinder Odysseus in his journey home. Hermes, the messenger god, is one of the first to help him. Tying golden sandals to his feet and retrieving his wand, he skims over the water to Ogygia, where Calypso agrees to release Odysseus.

She gives him bread, water, wine and clothes and instructs him to build himself a raft. These are his tools: a large, bronze-headed axe with olive-wood handle; an adze; a borer; nails; bands for joining; flexible willow branches; cloth for a sail; and alder, black poplar and pine, which he must cut down himself.

Homer often describes Odysseus as 'resourceful' or 'of many ways'. He is intellectually and physically agile. The raft he builds himself is so strong that he can drift over the sea for seventeen days. On the eighteenth, however, just as he comes within sight of land, he is struck by a gale stirred up by Poseidon. This is disastrous, for in Homer, no glory can come to those who drown. The prospect of dying such a dishonourable death makes Odysseus wish he had fallen at Troy.

Ingeniously, however, Odysseus clambers on to a single beam as if it were a horse, strips off his clothes and ties around his chest a magic veil a sea goddess gives him for his protection. He swims for land but is flung against a jagged rock and clings on: 'As when an octopus is drawn out of its lair and bits of pebble get stuck in its suckers, so his skin was stripped from his brave hands by the rock.'

The importance of hospitality

Of all the Homeric heroes, Odysseus is perhaps the easiest to identify with because, though highly skilled, he is also an everyman. He appeals to us because he shows that we can succeed in spite of the occasional failing if we sacrifice selfish pleasure to a greater purpose. The greatest temptation awaits him when he finally emerges from Poseidon's sea storm and reaches land at a place called Scheria (probably modern Corfu). Concealing his nakedness with leaves, he encounters some girls playing ball, among them a thoughtful princess named Nausicaa, who directs him to her family home. Her father, Alcinous, king of the Phaeacians, lives in a palace with bronze walls, gold doors and silver doorposts with dogs cast from gold and silver on either side. There is something immortal about this place, for the pears, pomegranates, shining apples, figs and olives in the palace orchard never spoil. Will Odysseus ever want to leave?

In the Homeric world, it is incumbent upon hosts to show 'xenia', 'hospitality', to strangers. It is proper to invite a man into one's home and give him food, and only then ask him about himself. The people of Scheria abide by these rules. A passage that recurs often in Homer – evidence of the poems' oral tradition – details the process. After Odysseus has entered the palace, a woman brings him a basin to wash from and pulls up a table, and another servant brings him bread and food. Only later does Odysseus reveal himself for who he is and tell stories of his travels since leaving Troy.

The Cyclops

Odysseus takes over from Homer in narrating his story over several books of the *Odyssey*. No other character speaks at such length. The pace of the narrative quickens as he tells his hosts of the Lotus Eaters, who fed his men lotus which made them forget their homecoming. And of the Sirens, whose song would have made him do the same had his men not tied him fast to their ship's mast as he listened to it. And of the one-eyed giants, the Cyclopes, who kept sheep and goats and made cheese from their milk.

Odysseus entertainingly recounts how he and twelve of his men entered the cave of a Cyclops named Polyphemus, ate his cheese and waited. The giant returned with his flock and closed the entrance to the cave behind him with a boulder so heavy that no man could move it. He proceeded to eat six of Odysseus' men. Odysseus devised a plan. He got the Cyclops drunk, told him his name was 'Nobody', blinded him with a cudgel and left the cave with his surviving men by clinging to the undersides of the sheep as they were put out to pasture. 'No one's killing you by trickery or force, are they?' the other Cyclopes asked Polyphemus when they heard his cry. 'Dear friends, Nobody is killing me by trickery or force,' he replied. He was left to suffer.

In the narrative of the poem the story of the Cyclops provides an explanation for Poseidon's hatred of Odysseus. The Cyclops Polyphemus is his son. If it was inevitable that Poseidon would punish him as he proceeded across the 'wine-coloured sea' on his raft, Odysseus only made the situation worse for himself by mocking the wounded Cyclops as he left. Odysseus is a fallible hero.

The inspiration for Odysseus' adventures

Odysseus' stories may be fantastic but they sometimes echo real developments in Greek history. The eighth century BCE was a time of exploration and sea travel. So it is that the Cyclopes are described in the poem as having no ships of their own in which to travel 'in the way that men often cross the sea by ship to one another'.

Like many Greeks of the eighth century BCE, Odysseus' hosts, the Phaeacians, are settlers. They are described as having come to Scheria after the Cyclopes terrorized them in their homeland. The contemporary world encroaches upon the Late Bronze Age in which the story is set when the Phaeacians are described as building temples to the gods.

The tales of Odysseus' travels were also inspired by stories which evolved over a thousand years earlier in the ancient Near East. The Mesopotamian *Epic of Gilgamesh* has a character named Ishtar, for example, who resembles Circe, a sorceress who turns some of Odysseus' men into pigs.

Odysseus is dispatched by Circe to meet the souls of the underworld. This scene provides closure to the war, for Odysseus encounters not only the soul of his mother, who died grieving for him, but also that of Achilles, who fell at Troy, and his comrade Ajax, who killed himself after losing a contest to win Achilles' armour – a contest Odysseus won. Unlike them, Odysseus is fated to survive. The Phaeacians, like the contemporary Greeks, are excellent sailors. They convey Odysseus home while he sleeps. (On their return, Poseidon vengefully turns their ship to stone.)

The test

The second half of the *Odyssey* is slower-moving than the first because there are so many elements of the story to be resolved. There is an emotional reunion between Odysseus and Telemachus after their respective travels. But Odysseus feels he needs to defeat the suitors before he can reveal himself to his wife, Penelope. On entering his home for the first time in twenty years, he therefore dons the disguise of a vagrant. His old nurse recognizes him when she washes him and sees the scar above his knee. Odysseus threatens to kill her if she breathes a word.

It is a strength of Homer's storytelling that he characterizes Odysseus as stalwart to the last. Far from softening in the domestic setting of Ithaca, as we might expect him to, Odysseus remains on his guard. Penelope now agrees to go away with whichever suitor can string Odysseus' bow and shoot an arrow through holes in twelve axes. Odysseus alone succeeds in the contest. Assisted by Athena, Telemachus and his loyal herdsmen, he turns arrows and spears against the suitors. Any servant girls who have slept with the suitors are hanged.

With a clever plot twist, Homer leaves us convinced that there is no other woman in the world for Odysseus than his wife. Penelope asks the nurse to put her bed outside. Odysseus is rattled. He built the bed himself around an olive tree so that its trunk formed one of the bedposts. It cannot be moved. A stranger could not possibly have known that. Through his reaction, Odysseus proves that he is who he says he is. He and Penelope go to bed together. After all his travels and travails, Odysseus has come home.

Homer's legacy

For centuries people have been searching for Homer and the truth behind his tales of the Trojan War. The sense of mystery that continues to shroud them has only contributed to their power. While the layering of elements from different periods and parts of the world makes the poems difficult to pin down, it also renders them truly timeless.

As readers we tend to feel this timelessness most palpably in the questions raised by the stories. How to confront death, how to accept fate, how to grieve, forgive, endure – it is comforting to believe that even heroes grappled with these issues. The challenges Odysseus had to overcome on returning to Ithaca are extreme but convey the struggle we all might face in settling back home after a long absence. This is what makes Homer so captivating.

Almost every poet in antiquity felt his influence. Virgil did for the Romans' history what Homer had done for the Greeks'; his epic poem, the *Aeneid*, celebrates the arrival in Italy of one of the refugees of the Trojan War. The Trojans came to be seen as the ancestors of the Roman people. Homer's poetry ran through their blood.

The legacy of Homer lives on in the work of many others, too, from the writings of Dante, Milton and James Joyce to the paintings of Rubens and J. M. W. Turner and the films of Mario Camerini and Wolfgang Petersen. His stories have been rewritten in almost every age and long may they continue to be. Homer may be ultimately unknowable – more a spirit than an individual – but he has achieved what his heroes always dreamed of. His name has become immortal.

Further reading

C. M. Bowra, *Homer* (Duckworth, 1972)

Paul Cartledge, *Ancient Greece: A Very Short Introduction* (Oxford University Press, 2011)

Robert Fowler (ed.), *The Cambridge Companion to Homer* (Cambridge University Press, 2004)

Barbara Graziosi, *Homer* (Oxford University Press, 2016)

Jasper Griffin, *Homer on Life and Death* (Clarendon Press, 1980); *Homer* (Bristol Classical Press, 2001)

Richard Jenkyns, *Classical Epic: Homer and Virgil* (Bristol Classical Press, 2004)

Machteld J. Mellink (ed.), *Troy and the Trojan War* (Bryn Mawr, 1999), especially the articles by M. Korfmann

Naoise Mac Sweeney, *Troy: Myth, City, Icon* (Bloomsbury Academic, 2018)

Ian Morris and Barry B. Powell (eds.), *A New Companion to Homer* (Brill, 1997)

Charles Brian Rose, *The Archaeology of Greek and Roman Troy* (Cambridge University Press, 2014)

Louise Schofield, *The Mycenaeans* (The British Museum Press, 2007)

Michael Silk, *Homer: The Iliad* (Cambridge University Press, 2004)

Sharon R. Steadman and Gregory McMahon (eds.), *The Oxford Handbook of Ancient Anatolia* (Oxford University Press, 2011)

Martin L. West, *Homeric Hymns, Homeric Apocrypha, Lives of Homer* (Harvard University Press, 2003)